Philip Glass

DOUBLE CONCERTO

DOUBLE CONCERTO

Duet No. 1

Philip Glass

♩ = 80

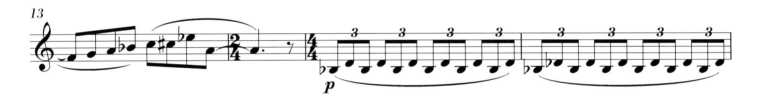

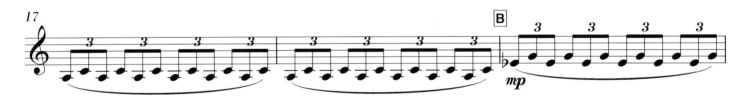

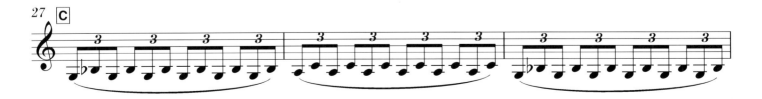

9/17/2010

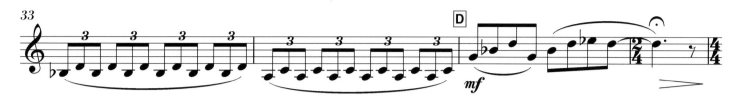

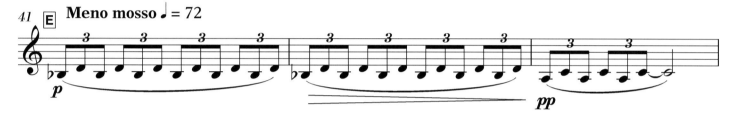

attacca

Part One

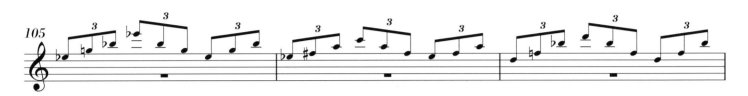

Blank for page turn.

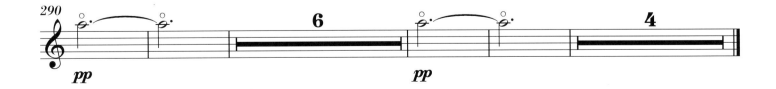

Duet No. 2

Part Two

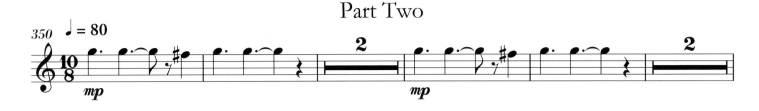

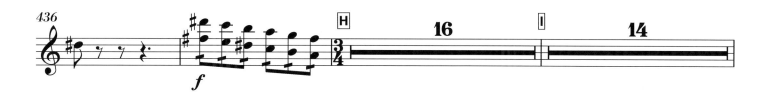

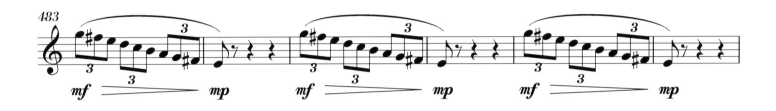

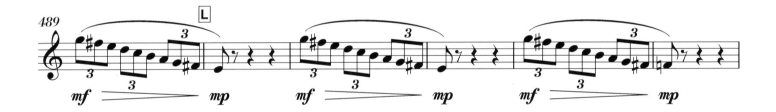

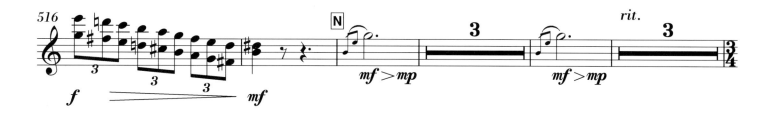

Duet No. 3

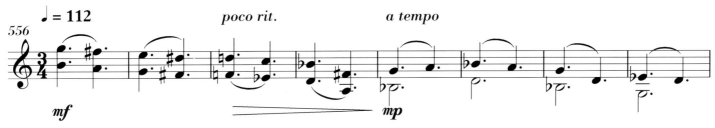

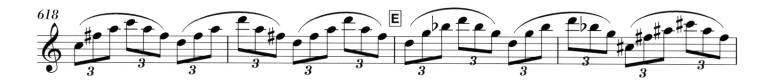

Part Three

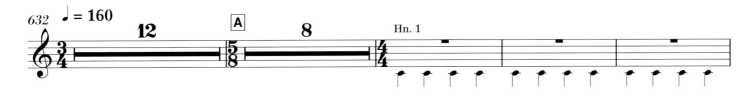

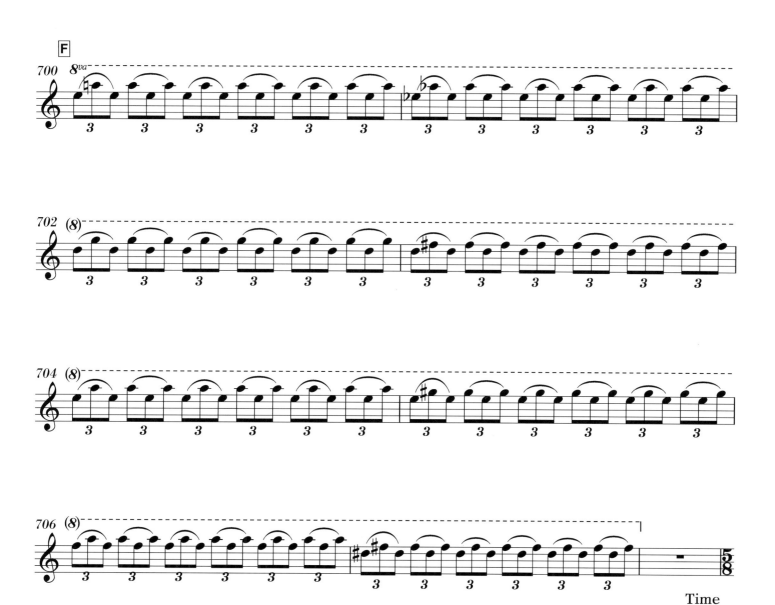

Time

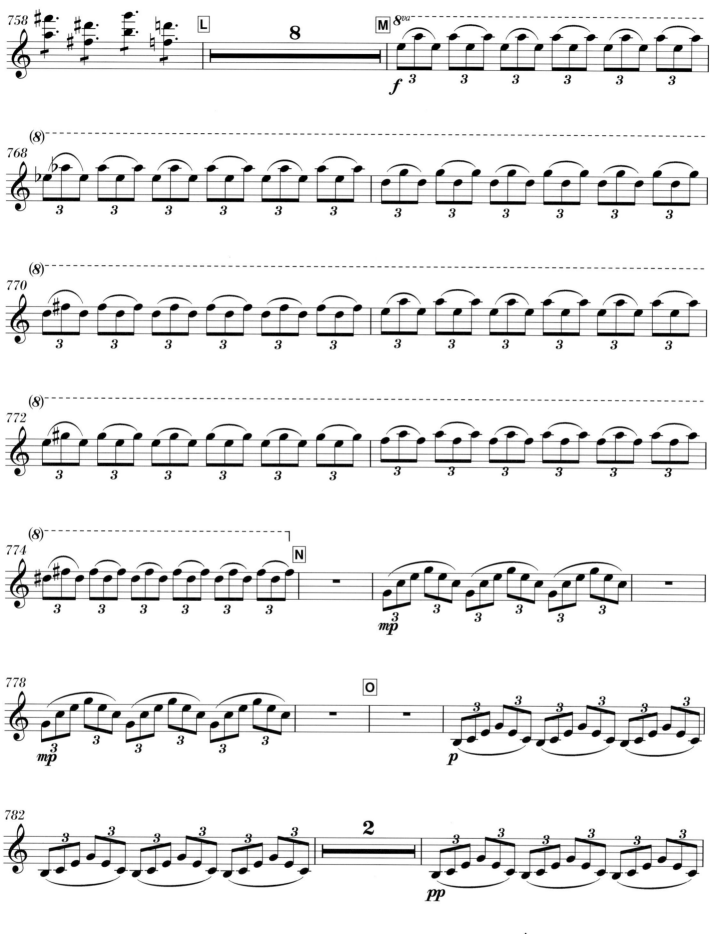

Solo Violin

Duet No. 4